Managing Human Resources

TEAM LEADING

Published for
The National Examining Board for Supervisory Management

by
Pergamon Open Learning
a division of
Pergamon Press Ltd
Oxford · New York · Seoul · Tokyo

U.K.	Pergamon Press plc, Headington Hill Hall, Oxford OX3 0BW, England
U.S.A.	Pergamon Press Inc, 660 White Plains Road, Tarrytown, New York 10591, NY, USA
KOREA	Pergamon Press Korea, KPO Box 315, Seoul 110-603, Korea
JAPAN	Pergamon Press, 8th Floor, Matsuoka Central Building, 1-7-1 Nishi-Shinjuku, Shinjuku-ku, Tokyo 160, Japan

This unit supersedes the Super Series first edition unit 103 (first edition 1986)

Second edition 1991
Reprinted 1992

A catalogue record for this book is available from the British Library

ISBN book and cassette kit: 0-08-041533-4

The views expressed in this work are those of the authors and do not necessarily reflect those of the National Examining Board for Supervisory Management or of the publisher.

Original text produced in conjunction with the Northern Regional Management Centre under an Open Tech Contract with the Manpower Services Commission.

Design and Production: Pergamon Open Learning

NEBSM Project Manager: Pam Sear

Author: Joe Johnson
First Edition Author: Ysanne Carlisle
Editor: Diana Thomas
Series Editor: Diana Thomas

Typeset by BPCC Techset Ltd, Exeter
Printed in Great Britain by BPCC Wheatons Ltd, Exeter

CONTENTS

USER GUIDE

1 Welcome to the User Guide

Hello and welcome to the NEBSM Super Series second edition (Super Series 2) flexible training programme.

It is quite likely that you are a supervisor, a team leader, an assistant manager, a foreman, a section head, a first-line or a junior manager and have people working under you. The Super Series programme is ideal for all, whatever the job title, who are on or near that first rung of the management ladder. By choosing this programme we believe that you have made exactly the right decision when it comes to meeting your own needs and those of your organization.

The purpose of this guide is to help you gain the maximum benefit both from this particular workbook and audio cassette and also from a full supervisory management training programme.

You should read the whole of this User Guide thoroughly before you start any work on the unit and use the information and advice to help plan your studies.

If you are new to the idea of studying or training by yourself or have never before worked with a tutor or trainer on an individual basis, you should pay particular attention to the section below about Open Learning and tutorial support.

If you are a trainer or tutor evaluating this material for use with prospective students or clients, we think you will also find the information given here useful as it will help you to prepare and conduct individual pre-course counselling and group briefing sessions.

2 Your Open Learning Programme

What do we mean by 'Open Learning'?

Let's start by looking at what is meant by 'Open Learning' and how it could affect the way you approach your studies.

Open Learning is a term used to describe a method of training where you, the learner, make most of the decisions about *how*, *when* and *where* you do your learning. To make this possible you need to have available material, written or prepared in a special way (such as this book and audio cassette) and then have access to Open Learning centres that have been set up and prepared to offer guidance and support as and when required.

Undertaking your self-development training by Open Learning allows you to fit in with priorities at work and at home and to build the right level of confidence and independence needed for success, even though at first it may take you a little while to establish a proper routine.

The workbook and audio cassette

Though this guide is mainly aimed at you as a first time user, it is possible that you are already familiar with the earlier editions of the Super Series. If that is the case, you should know that there are quite a few differences in the workbook and audio cassette, some of which were very successfully trialled in the last 12 units of the first edition. Apart from the more noticeable features such as changes in page layouts and more extensive use of colour and graphics, you will find activities, questions and assignments that are more closely related to work and more thought-provoking.

The amount of material on the cassette is, on average, twice the length of older editions and is considerably more integrated with the workbook. In fact, there are so many extras now that are included as standard that the average study time per unit has been increased by almost a third. You will find a useful summary of all workbook and cassette features in the charts below and on page vii.

Whether you are a first time user or not, the first step towards being a successful Open Learner is to be familiar and comfortable with the learning material. It is well worth spending a little of your initial study time scanning the workbook to see how it is structured, what the various sections and features are called and what they are designed to do.

This will save you a lot of time and frustration when you start studying as you will then be able to concentrate on the actual subject matter itself without the need to refer back to what you are supposed to be doing with each part.

At the outset you are assumed to have no prior knowledge or experience of the subject and can expect to be taken logically, step by step from start to finish of the learning programme. To help you take on new ideas and information, and to help you remember and apply them, you will come across many different and challenging self check tasks, activities, quizzes and questions which you should approach seriously and enthusiastically. These features are designed not only to make your learning easier and more interesting but to help you to apply what you are studying to your own work situation in a practical and down-to-earth way.

To help to scan the workbook and cassette properly, and to understand what you find, here is a summary of the main features:

The workbook

If you want:	Refer to:
To see which other Super Series 2 units can also help you with this topic	The Study links
An overview of every part of the workbook and how the book and audio cassette link together	The Unit map
A list of the main knowledge and skill outcomes you will gain from the unit	The Unit objectives
To check on your understanding of the subject and your progress as you work thorough each section	The Activities and Self checks
To test how much you have understood and learned of the whole unit when your studies are complete	The Quick quiz and Action checks
An assessment by a third party for work done and time spent on this unit for purposes of recognition, award or certification	The Unit assessment The Work-based assignment
To put some of the things learned from the unit into practice in your own work situation	The Action plan (where present)

If you want:	Refer to:
To start your study of the unit	The Introduction: Side one
To check your knowledge of the complete unit	The Quick quiz: Side one
To check your ability to apply what you have learned to 'real life' by listening to some situations and deciding what you should do or say	The Action checks: Side two

Managing your learning programme

When you feel you know your way around the material, and in particular appreciate the progress checking and assessment features, the next stage is to put together your own personal study plan and decide how best to study.

These two things are just as important as checking out the material; they are also useful time savers and give you the satisfaction of feeling organized and knowing exactly where you are going and what you are trying to achieve.

You have already chosen your subject (this unit) so you should now decide when you need to finish the unit and how much time you must spend to make sure you reach your target.

To help you to answer these questions, you should know that each workbook and audio cassette will probably take about *eight* to *ten* hours to complete; the variation in time allows for different reading, writing and study speeds and the length and complexity of any one subject.

Don't be concerned if it takes you longer than these average times, especially on your first unit, and always keep in mind that the objective of your training is understanding and applying the learning, not competing in a race.

Experience has shown that each unit is best completed over a two-week period with about *three* to *four* study hours spent on it in each week, and about *one* to *two* hours at each sitting. These times are about right for tackling a new subject and still keeping work and other commitments sensibly in balance.

Using these time guides you should set, and try to keep to, specific times, days, and dates for your study. You should write down what you have decided and keep it visible as a reminder. If you are studying more than one unit, probably as part of a larger training programme, then the compilation of a full, dated plan or schedule becomes even more important and might have to tie in with dates and times set by others, such as a tutor.

The next step is to decide where to study. If you are doing this training in conjunction with your company or organization this might be decided for you as most have quiet areas, training rooms, learning centres, etc., which you will be encouraged to use. If you are working at home, set aside a quiet corner where books and papers can be left and kept together with a comfortable chair and a simple writing surface. You will also need a note pad and access to cassette playing equipment.

When you are finally ready to start studying, presuming that you are feeling confident and organized after your preparations, you should follow the instructions given in the Unit Map and the Unit Objectives pages. These tell you to play the first part of Side one of the audio cassette, a couple of times is a good idea, then follow the cues back to the workbook.

You should then work through each workbook section doing all that is asked of you until you reach the final assessments. Don't forget to keep your eye on the Unit Map as you progress and try to finish each session at a sensible point in the unit, ideally at the end of a complete section or part. You should always start your next session by looking back, for at least ten to fifteen minutes, at the work you did in the previous session.

You are encouraged to retain any reports, work-based assignments or other material produced in conjunction with your work through this unit in case you wish to present these later as evidence for a competency award or accreditation of prior learning.

Help, guidance and tutorial support

The workbook and audio cassette have been designed to be as self-contained as possible, acting as your guide and tutor throughout your studies. However, there are bound to be times when you might not quite understand what the author is saying, or perhaps you don't agree with a certain point. Whatever the reason, we all need help and support from time to time and Open Learners are no exception.

Help during Open Learning study can come in many forms, providing you are prepared to seek it out and use it:

● first of all you could help yourself. Perhaps you are giving up too easily. Go back over it and try again;

● or you could ask your family or friends. Even if they don't understand the subject, the act of discussing it sometimes clarifies things in your own mind;

● then there is your company trainer or superior. If you are training as part of a company scheme, and during work time, then help and support will probably have been arranged for you already. Help and advice under these circumstances are important, especially as they can help you interpret your studies through actual and relevant company examples;

● if you are pursuing this training on your own, you could enlist expert help from a local Open Learning centre or agency. Such organizations exist in considerable numbers throughout the UK, often linked to colleges and other training establishments. The National Examining Board for Supervisory Management (NEBSM or NEBS Management), has several hundred such centres and can provide not only help and support but full assessment and accreditation facilities if you want to pursue a qualification as part of your chosen programme.

The NEBSM Super Series second edition is a selection of workbook and audio cassette packages covering a wide range of supervisory and first line management topics.

Although the individual books and cassettes are completely self-contained and cover single subject areas, each belongs to one of the four modular groups shown. These groups can help you build up your personal development programme as you can easily see which subjects are related. The groups are also important if you undertake any NEBSM national award programme.

Managing Human Resources

HR1	Supervising at Work	HR10	Managing Time
HR2	Supervising with Authority	HR11	Hiring People
HR3	Team Leading	HR12	Interviewing
HR4	Delegation	HR13	Training Plans
HR5	Workteams	HR14	Training Sessions
HR6	Motivating People	HR15	Industrial Relations
HR7	Leading Change	HR16	Employment and the Law
HR8	Personnel in Action	HR17	Equality at Work
HR9	Performance Appraisal	HR18	Work-based Assessment

Managing Information

IN1	Communicating	IN7	Using Statistics
IN2	Speaking Skills	IN8	Presenting Figures
IN3	Orders and Instructions	IN9	Introduction to
IN4	Meetings		Information Technology
IN5	Writing Skills	IN10	Computers and
IN6	Project Preparation		Communication Systems

Managing Financial Resources

FR1	Accounting for Money	FR4	Pay Systems
FR2	Control via Budgets	FR5	Security
FR3	Controlling Costs		

Managing Products and Services

PS1	Controlling Work	PS8	Productivity
PS2	Health and Safety	PS9	Stock Control Systems
PS3	Accident Prevention	PS10	Stores Control
PS4	Ensuring Quality	PS11	Efficiency in the Office
PS5	Quality Techniques	PS12	Marketing
PS6	Taking Decisions	PS13	Caring for the Environment
PS7	Solving Problems	PS14	Caring for the Customer

While the contents have been thoroughly updated, many Super Series 2 titles remain the same as, or very similar to the first edition units. Where, through merger, rewrite or deletion title changes have also been made, this summary should help you. If you are in any doubt please contact Pergamon Open Learning direct.

First Edition

Merged titles
105 Organization Systems and 106 Supervising in the System
100 Needs and Rewards and 101 Enriching Work
502 Discipline and the Law and 508 Supervising and the Law
204 Easy Statistics and 213 Descriptive Statistics
200 Looking at Figures and 202 Using Graphs
210 Computers and 303 Communication Systems

402 Cost Reduction and 405 Cost Centres
203 Method Study and 208 Value Analysis

Major title changes
209 Quality Circles
205 Quality Control

Deleted titles
406 National Economy/410 Single European Market

Second Edition

HR1 Supervising at Work
HR6 Motivating People
HR16 Employment and the Law
IN7 Using Statistics
IN8 Presenting Figures
IN10 Computers and Communication Systems
FR3 Controlling Costs
PS8 Productivity

PS4 Ensuring Quality
PS5 Quality Techniques

The NEBSM Super Series 2 Open Learning material is published by Pergamon Open Learning in conjunction with NEBS Management.

NEBS Management is the largest provider of management education, training courses and qualifications in the United Kingdom, operating through over 700 Centres. Many of these Centres offer Open Learning and can provide help to individual students.

Many thousands of students follow the Open Learning route with great success and gain NEBSM or other qualifications.

NEBSM maintains a twin track approach to Supervisory Management training offering knowledge-based awards at three levels:

- the NEBSM Introductory Award in Supervisory Management;
- the NEBSM Certificate in Supervisory Management;
- the NEBSM Diploma in Supervisory Management;

and competence based awards at two levels:

- the NEBSM NVQ in Supervisory Management at Level 3;
- the NEBSM NVQ in Management at Level 4.

Knowledge-based awards and Super Series 2

The ***Introductory Award*** requires a minimum of 30 hours of study and provides a grounding in the theory and practice of supervisory management. An agreed programme of up to five NEBSM Super Series 2 units plus a one-day workshop satisfactorily completed can lead to this Award. Pre-approved topic combinations exist for general, industrial and commercial options. Completed Super Series 2 units can be allowed as an exemption towards the full NEBSM Certificate.

The ***Certificate in Supervisory Management*** requires study of up to 23 NEBSM Super Series 2 units and participation in group activity or workshops. The assessment system includes work-based assignments, a case study, a project and an oral interview. The certificate is divided into four modules and each one may be completed separately. A ***Module Award*** can be made on successful completion of each module, and when the assessments are satisfactorily completed the Certificate is awarded. Students will need to register with a NEBSM Centre in order to enter for an award; NEBSM can advise you.

The ***Diploma in Supervisory Management*** consists of the formulation and implementation of a Personal Development Plan plus a generic management core. The programme is assessed by means of a log book, case study/in tray exercises, project or presentation.

The NEBSM Super Series 2 Open Learning material is designed for use at Certificate level but can also be used for the Introductory Award and provide valuable background knowledge for the Diploma.

Competence-based programmes and Super Series 2

The ***NEBSM NVQ in Supervisory Management Level 3*** is based upon the seven units of competence produced by the Management Charter Initiative (MCI) in their publication *Supervisory Management Standards* of June 1992. It is recognized by the National Council for Vocational Qualifications (NCVQ) at Level 3 in their framework.

The ***NEBSM NVQ in Management Level 4*** is based upon the nine units of competence produced by MCI in their publication *Occupational Standards for Managers, Management 1 and Assessment Criteria* of April 1991. It is recognized by the National Council for Vocational Qualifications (NCVQ) at Level 4 in their framework.

Super Series 2 units can be used to provide the necessary underpinning knowledge, skills and understanding that are required to prepare yourself for competence-based assessment.

Working through Super Series 2 units cannot, by itself, provide you with everything you need to enter or be entered for competence assessment. This must come from a combination of skill, experience and knowledge gained both on and off the job.

You will also find many of the 47 Super Series 2 units of use in learning programmes for other National Vocational Qualifications (NVQs) which include elements of supervisory management. Please check with the relevant NVQ lead body for information on Units of Competence and underlying knowledge, skills and understanding.

Competence Match Chart

The Competence Match Chart overleaf illustrates which Super Series 2 titles provide background vital to the current MCI M1S Supervisory Management Standards. You will also find that there is similar matching at MCI M1, Management 1 Standards. This is shown on the chart on page xiii.

For more information about MCI contact:

Management Charter Initiative
Russell Square House
10–12 Russell Square
London
WC1B 5BZ

Progression

Many successful NEBSM students use their qualifications as stepping stones to other awards, both educational and professional. Recognition is given by a number of bodies for this purpose. Further details about this and other NEBSM matters can be obtained from:

NEBSM Information Officer
The National Examining Board for Supervisory Management
76 Portland Place
London
W1N 4AA

Competence Match Chart MCI M1S

The chart shows matches of Super Series 2 titles with MCI M1S (Supervisory Management) Units of Competence. Titles indicated ● are directly relevant to MCI Units, those marked ◐ provide specific supporting information, and those listed ○ provide useful general background.

NEBSM Super Series 2 Titles — **MCI M1 S Units of Competence (see below)**

		1	2	3	4	5	6	7
PS1	Controlling Output	◐	◐					
PS2	Health and Safety	●	○			○		
PS3	Accident Prevention	●	○			○		
PS4	Ensuring Quality	●	○					
PS5	Quality Techniques	●						
PS6	Taking Decisions	○	○			◐	◐	
PS7	Solving Problems	○	○			◐	●	
PS8	Productivity		◐			●		
PS9	Stock Control Systems		◐					
PS10	Stores Control		◐					
PS11	Efficiency in the Office		◐			◐		
PS12	Marketing	○						
PS13	Caring for the Environment	◐	◐			○	○	○
PS14	Caring for the Customer	◐	○			○		
HR1	Supervising at Work					●	●	
HR2	Supervising with Authority					●	●	
HR3	Team Leading					●	●	
HR4	Delegation				●	●	◐	
HR5	Workteams					●	●	
HR6	Motivating People					●	●	
HR7	Leading Change		◐			●		
HR8	Personnel in Action			●				
HR9	Performance Appraisal				●		●	
HR10	Managing Time		○		○			
HR11	Hiring People			●				
HR12	Interviewing			●	●	◐	●	
HR13	Training Plans				●			
HR14	Training Sessions				●			
HR15	Industrial Relations						●	
HR16	Employment and the Law			○			●	
HR17	Equality at Work			◐			●	
HR18	Work-based Assessment			○	●	●	○	○
FR1	Accounting for Money		●					
FR2	Control via Budgets		●					
FR3	Controlling Costs		●					
FR4	Pay Systems							
FR5	Security	◐	◐					
IN1	Communicating	○	○	○	○	○	○	●
IN2	Speaking Skills	○	○	○	○	○	○	●
IN3	Orders and Instructions	◐				●	●	
IN4	Meetings				○	●	◐	●
IN5	Writing Skills	○	◐			○	◐	○
IN6	Project Preparation				○			
IN7	Using Statistics	◐	◐					●
IN8	Presenting Figures	◐	◐					●
IN9	Introduction to Information Technology	◐	◐					●
IN10	Computers and Communication Systems	◐	◐					●

* MCI M1 S. Units of Competence

1. Maintain services and operations to meet quality standards
2. Contribute to the planning, monitoring and control of resources
3. Contribute to the provision of personnel
4. Contribute to the training and development of teams, individuals and self to enhance performance
5. Contribute to the planning, organization and evaluation of work
6. Create, maintain and enhance productive working relationships
7. Provide information and advice for action towards meeting organizational objectives

Competence Match Chart MCI M1

The chart indicates the Super Series 2 titles which provide some useful background information to support MCI M1 (Management level 1) Units of Competence.

NEBSM Super Series 2 Titles		1	2	3	4	5	6	7	8	9
PS1	Controlling Output	△	△							
PS2	Health and Safety	△								
PS3	Accident Prevention	△								
PS4	Ensuring Quality	△	△							
PS5	Quality Techniques	△	△							
PS6	Taking Decisions								△	△
PS7	Solving Problems		△						△	△
PS8	Productivity		△							
PS9	Stock Control Systems	△								
PS10	Stores Control	△								
PS11	Efficiency in the Office	△	△							
PS12	Marketing	△								
PS13	Caring for the Environment	△								
PS14	Caring for the Customer		△							
HR1	Supervising at Work							△		
HR2	Supervising with Authority							△		△
HR3	Team Leading					△	△	△		
HR4	Delegation					△	△	△		
HR5	Workteams					△	△	△		△
HR6	Motivating People							△		
HR7	Leading Change		△							
HR8	Personnel in Action				△					
HR9	Performance Appraisal							△		
HR10	Managing Time									
HR11	Hiring People				△					
HR12	Interviewing				△	△		△		
HR13	Training Plans					△				
HR14	Training Sessions					△				
HR15	Industrial Relations							△		
HR16	Employment and the Law				△			△		
HR17	Equality at Work				△			△		
HR18	Work-based Assessment					△	△			
FR1	Accounting for Money			△						
FR2	Control via Budgets			△						
FR3	Controlling Costs			△						
FR4	Pay Systems									
FR5	Security									
IN1	Communicating							△		△
IN2	Speaking Skills			△				△		△
IN3	Orders and Instructions							△		△
IN4	Meetings							△		△
IN5	Writing Skills			△			△	△		△
IN6	Project Preparation			△			△	△		
IN7	Using Statistics							△	△	△
IN8	Presenting Figures							△	△	△
IN9	Introduction to Information Technology								△	△
IN10	Computers and Communication Systems								△	△

* MCI M1 Units of Competence

Key Role: Manage Operations
— 1. Maintain and improve service and product operations
— 2. Contribute to the implementation of change in services, products and systems

Key Role: Manage Finance
— 3. Recommend, monitor and control the use of resources

Key Role: Manage People
— 4. Contribute to the recruitment and selection of personnel
— 5. Develop teams, individuals and self to enhance performance
— 6. Plan, allocate and evaluate work carried out by teams, individuals and self
— 7. Create, maintain and enhance effective working relationships

Key Role: Manage Information
— 8. Seek, evaluate and organise information for action
— 9. Exchange information to solve problems and make decisions

Guide | Unit Completion Certificate

Completion of this Certificate by an authorized and qualified person indicates that you have worked through all parts of this unit and completed all assessments. If you are studying this unit as part of a certificated programme, or think you may wish to in future, then completion of this Certificate is particularly important as it may be used for exemptions, credit accumulation or Accreditation of Prior Learning (APL). Full details can be obtained from NEBSM.

NEBSM
SUPER SERIES
Second Edition

HR3

Team leading

. . . .

has satisfactorily completed this unit.

Name of Signatory. . . . .
Position. . . . .
Signature. . . . .

                    Date . . . .

Official Stamp

Keep in touch

Pergamon Open Learning and NEBS Management are always happy to hear of your experiences of using the Super Series to help improve supervisory and managerial effectiveness. This will assist us with continuous product improvement, and novel approaches and success stories may be included in promotional information to illustrate to others what can be done.

1 NEBSM Super Series 2 study links

Here are the Super Series 2 units which link with *Team Leading*. You may find this useful when you are putting together your study programme but you should bear in mind that:

● each Super Series 2 unit stands alone and does not depend upon being used in conjunction with any other unit;

● Super Series 2 units can be used in any order which suits your learning needs.

WORKTEAMS
Analyzes just what make a good workteam, what the individuals contribute and how a team develops.

ORDERS AND INSTRUCTIONS
Giving your team clear instructions is an important leadership skill.

MOTIVATING PEOPLE
Shows what satisfaction your workteam looks for at work and how you can help provide it.

TEAM LEADING
How to build, lead and maintain a team and ensure that it works effectively.

SUPERVISING IN THE SYSTEM
All about harmonizing your work and that of your team within the organization as a whole.

LEADING CHANGE
Heading your team to meet the opportunities of change and coping with any threats or problems.

SUPERVISING WITH AUTHORITY
Helps to identify and use the authority you need to lead and maintain your team.

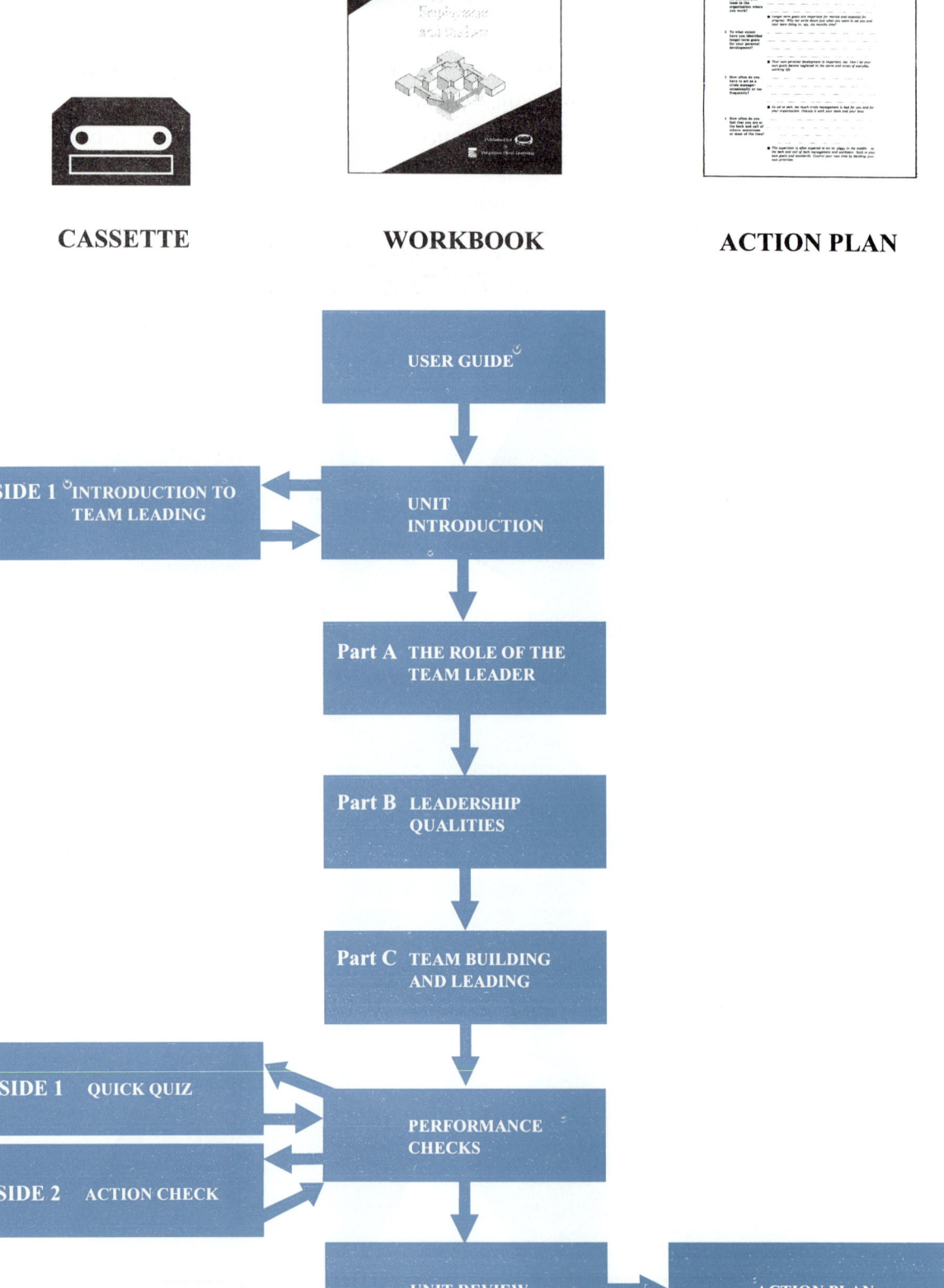

CASSETTE   WORKBOOK   ACTION PLAN

USER GUIDE

SIDE 1 INTRODUCTION TO TEAM LEADING → UNIT INTRODUCTION

Part A THE ROLE OF THE TEAM LEADER

Part B LEADERSHIP QUALITIES

Part C TEAM BUILDING AND LEADING

SIDE 1 QUICK QUIZ

SIDE 2 ACTION CHECK

PERFORMANCE CHECKS

UNIT REVIEW → ACTION PLAN

Team leaders are special people. They have the key task of making things happen – of implementing the plans of higher management by organizing and motivating the teams they represent.

What we will try to do in this unit is to examine ways in which you, as a team leader, can improve your leadership skills and techniques, and so become more effective.

Before you start work on this unit, listen carefully to Side one of the accompanying audio cassette which sets the scene for your examination of *Team Leading*.

In this unit we will:

- look at the role of the team leader in the organization;
- examine and analyse the management aspects of team leading;
- identify the qualities and attributes of a good leader;
- discuss the formation and development of a team.

Objectives

When you have worked through this unit you will be ***better able to:***

- identify your role in the organization and your relationship with others;
- recognize and develop the management skills you need to lead a team;
- assess your own leadership qualities and potential;
- lead your team effectively.

THE ROLE OF THE TEAM LEADER

1   Introduction

A lot is expected of a team leader. If you have already led a team you will know that people look to you to be both resourceful and independent. The team demands your loyalty and so does the organization. Yet, when things aren't going well, you get the impression that there are many who are ready to blame you for the mistakes of others.

But the job has its compensations. Being a team leader is nearly always challenging and often very rewarding. It is seldom boring!

In this part of the unit we start by looking at where the team leader fits into the organization as a whole.

Then we examine the responsibilities and the rewards of running a team.

We next investigate the stress which can result from the various roles played by team leaders and team members, and how to deal with it.

In the last section we go into the management aspects of team leadership.

2.1
The changes that promotion brings

Activity 1

■ Time guide 5 minutes

Margaret Brown has been a member of a workteam for the past five years. She likes the job and gets on well with other members of the team.

One Monday morning Margaret gets a message that her Department Manager wants to see her. When she goes to his office, the Personnel Officer is also there.

Margaret is told that a number of vacancies for supervisory positions will soon arise and that she has been recommended as a suitable person for promotion. If she wants the job, Margaret will be promoted to team leader.

Naturally, Margaret needs time to think about this proposal. Later, she sits down to try to think about all the implications of the change.

Put yourself in Margaret's shoes. Jot down *two* or ***three*** ways in which promotion to team leader might be expected to alter life at work.

_____

_____

_____

_____

_____

_____

Anyone being promoted from being in a team to being team leader can expect a number of fairly fundamental changes. It might be said that this step is a critical turning point in a person's working life – perhaps a change requiring more adjustment than many later promotions!

Among the changes are:

■ your relationships with colleagues: suddenly you are no longer 'one of the girls' (or boys) in the workteam, but a member of a different team – the management team of the organization;

■ how you spend your working day: in a sense you will no longer be paid for the work that you do because ***you have to get things done through other people rather than doing them yourself;***

■ the amount of responsibility you have: a team leader has many more obligations and concerns;

■ the increased status;

■ where you fit into the organization.

This last point is an important one. When you are promoted to team leader your place in the organization changes. You need to start by looking at your relationships with others and where you fit in.

Let's look more closely at the structure of organizations.

As you may know, 'official' relationships and status can be represented on an *organization chart*. One such chart is as shown below:

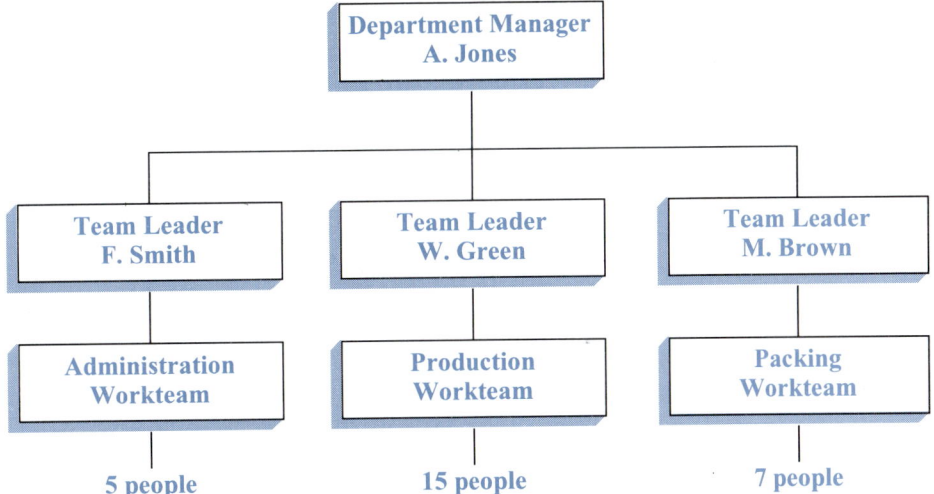

The chart above shows a typical organization structure in which:

- the Manager, A. Jones, is responsible for the whole department;
- the department is split into three workteams, each of which is headed by a team leader;
- each team leader has the authority to run a particular workteam;
- each team leader reports to the manager for the particular task allocated to the workteam.

In this structure, team leaders report to only one manager. Other arrangements are possible. Sometimes, the structure may require teams to be assigned to particular project managers, while still reporting to the line manager for administrative purposes. A typical example of this 'matrix' structure is shown below.

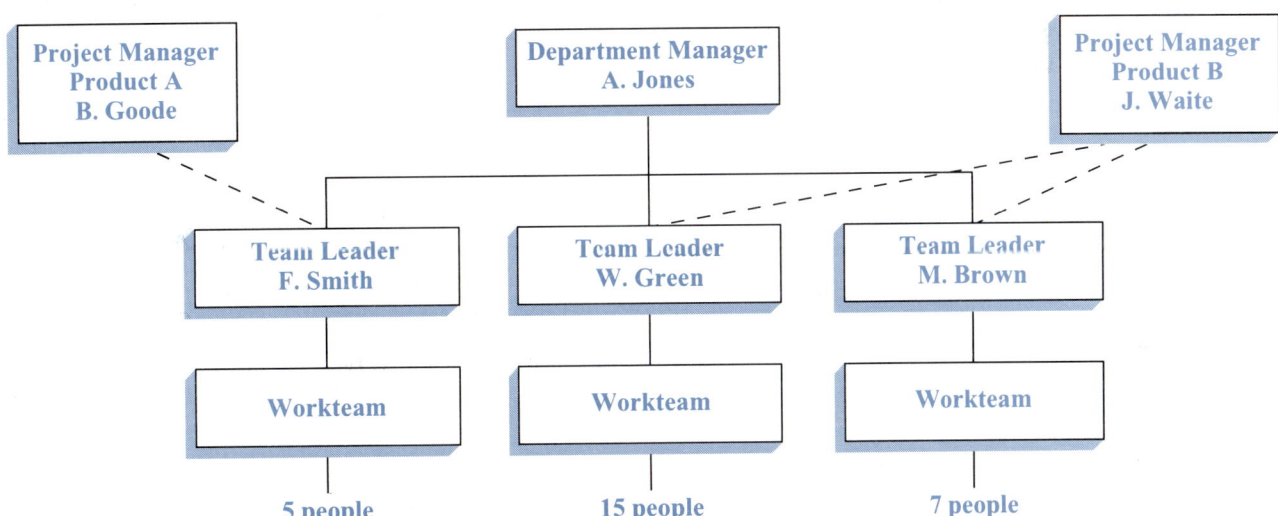

In this diagram, the three team leaders report to the Department Manager for administration purposes. Two of the teams (W. Green's and M. Brown's) work on the project run by J. Waite. The other team (F. Smith's) work on the project run by B. Goode. Thus the team leaders each report to two managers.

Activity 2

■ Time guide 15 minutes

Are you aware of where you fit in to your own organization? Sketch out the part of the organization chart which covers your own job. You could start by putting down your name and position and drawing lines to the people you report to and the people who report to you. Then put in groups equivalent to yours, which report to the same person. Include any others with whom you or your group have official contact.

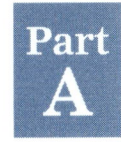

If you can, compare your version of the organizational structure with the approved version. If not, ask your boss if he or she thinks your sketch is accurate.

2.3 Informal structure

Of course, if you were to trace out all the lines of contact or communication, official and unofficial, between you and others in the organization, your chart could become very complicated. You may have casual contact with a great many people, such as: members of other teams and departments, typists and secretaries, union representatives, sports club members and so on.

There are always a number of *informal* groupings within any organisation, as well as the *formal* ones.

Informal relationships between people are often just as important as the formal ones.

'If we had an ultrasonic cleaner we could do a good job on reconditioning those parts.' Perry Brady was talking over a problem with Ned, one of his team. 'But there's none in stores and we'll never get hold of one in time now.'

'I know where there's one,' said Ned. 'I've got a pal in D Division over the road and I know for a fact that they've got two not being used.'

'Ned, you may have saved the day. I'll contact the manager right away.'

We've all had experiences of this kind. In most organizations the information flow through the formal hierarchy is not entirely efficient;

informal groupings can provide short-cuts to achievement.

**3.1
The responsibilities**

Activity 3

> ■ Time guide 5 minutes
>
> Read this account of a supervisor's interview with her boss, and then say what you think about it.
>
> *Hannah wasn't happy. She had taken over as supervisor of a team of process operators in a company making small assemblies, nine months before. She thought she had been doing well, but was rather disappointed in the annual merit pay rise she had received. Hannah asked to see her boss and said to him:*
>
> *'When I took over this team, morale was low, things were badly organized and most of the people on the team were not properly trained for the jobs they were doing.'*
>
> *Hannah then went on to give an account of all the work she had done to improve things, since she had taken over the running of the team. Hannah's boss heard her out patiently, and then said:*
>
> *'It's true that you have done very well, Hannah, and I agree with what you say. However, the fact remains that the output and quality of your team's work is still below the others. We want people to be happy and trained and well motivated. All these things are important. But you musn't forget that your team has been set up in order to help us manufacture high quality goods at an economic rate.'*
>
> From what you've read of the case, do you think Hannah's boss is justified in criticizing her in this way? Jot down your views in the space below.
>
> _____
>
> _____
>
> _____
>
> _____
>
> _____
>
> _____

Without knowing any more about the details, I think I'd broadly agree with the points made by Hannah's boss. Achievement of the main task is the team leader's prime responsibility, because ***the allotted task is the reason for the workteam's existence: all other considerations are secondary***.

It is the team leader to whom management will look for ensuring that the team's task is accomplished. And it is to the team leader that the team will look to guide them through the difficulties of achieving the task.

Achievement of the task
is the team leader's main responsibility.

Of course, there are other responsibilities, as we've already hinted. Among these is a ***responsibility towards individuals***.

Activity 4

■ Time guide 5 minutes

What does 'responsibility towards individuals' mean, do you think?

Read the following account, and jot down any points which it suggests to you about the responsibilities of the team leader towards the individuals in a team.

John Spicer was a social worker, employed by a local authority. When John's new supervisor, Mary Harrison, was appointed, John was glad of the opportunity to have a long chat with her. Mary encouraged John to speak freely about his problems. Here's an extract of what John had to say:

'Before you came, Mary, we were left very much to our own devices. We got very little support and not much encouragement. As you know, this job can be very tough at times. I've been physically attacked on a couple of occasions for instance, by the very people I was trying to help. Also, I know people in the team who have been given jobs which they had had no training or preparation for. What's more, there isn't any proper system of reviewing objectives or performance, so we don't know how well we've been doing or what is expected of us.'

_____

_____

_____

_____

_____

You may have noticed that John made several points which remind us about the responsibility of team leaders towards individuals. These include:

■ *supporting the individual* with help and advice;

■ *encouraging and motivating*;

■ *assigning jobs appropriate to the member's abilities*;

■ *making clear the job roles of the team members*, so that everyone knows what is expected of them;

■ *assessing performance*;

■ perhaps *protecting the individual* from other people, including other members of the group.

Another responsibility is towards *the team as a whole*. The team is made up of people and yet it also has an identity of its own.

Activity 5

■ Time guide 4 minutes

Apart from the responsibilities towards individuals that we listed above, what are the leader's responsibilities towards the team as a whole?

One example is 'demonstrating a total commitment to the task and the team'. Try to list *three* other points.

_____

_____

_____

_____

_____

_____

You may agree that the team leader is responsible for:

■ *defining the group task*, purpose or goal, and explaining it to the group, so that everyone knows what has to be done and why it has to be done;

■ *co-ordinating the team's efforts*;

■ *blending the skills and attributes of individuals into an integrated whole*;

■ *ensuring the standards of the group are maintained*;

■ *helping the team achieve its common task*;

■ *supporting the team* when things are going wrong.

In summary, then,

the team leader has responsibilities towards
the task, the team and the individual.

Yet another set of responsibilities concerns the relationship of the team to other groups. The team leader is also charged with:

■ representing the team to management;

■ representing management to the team;

■ co-ordinating with other teams and departments.

This can be shown in the form of a diagram:

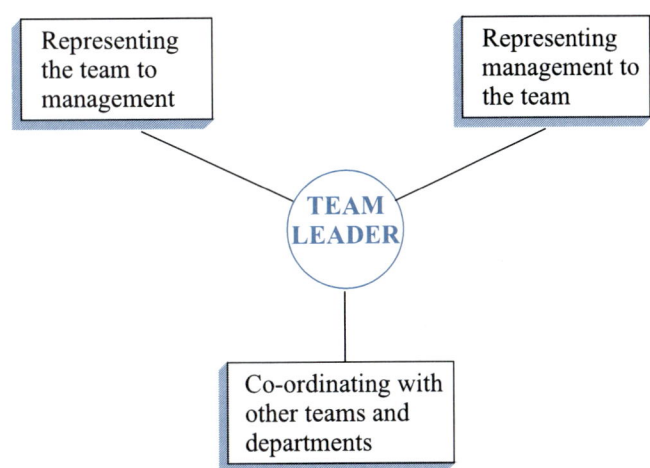

Taking on all these responsibilities can be a rather daunting prospect for the newly appointed leader. A team leader's or supervisor's job is not an easy one. However, there are compensations.

**3.2
The benefits**

Activity 6

■ Time guide 3 minutes

What about the benefits? What advantages are there to an individual who is promoted to the position of team leader? Jot down *two* benefits which you might hope to receive.

_____

_____

_____

_____

The benefits of promotion vary, depending on the job.

■ By definition, promotion means *higher status* within the organisation.

■ It may also bring a rise in pay and other *financial rewards*.

■ Almost certainly a team leader will have a *greater influence* on the way things are done than an ordinary team member will.

■ There will also be *more involvement*.

■ There may well be *greater job satisfaction*.

A

4.1
The roles we play

So far, we've covered:

● *relationships* – the position of the team leader in the organization;

● *responsibilities* – what the team leader is answerable for.

Another way of looking at these two concepts is in terms of the *roles* the team leader plays.

Extension 1 Effective Teambuilding by John Adair is a useful source of information on all aspects of role playing. In addition it covers several other aspects of our subject.

If you were to draw a simple chart of your interactions with other people, both inside and outside work, a simplified version might look something like this:

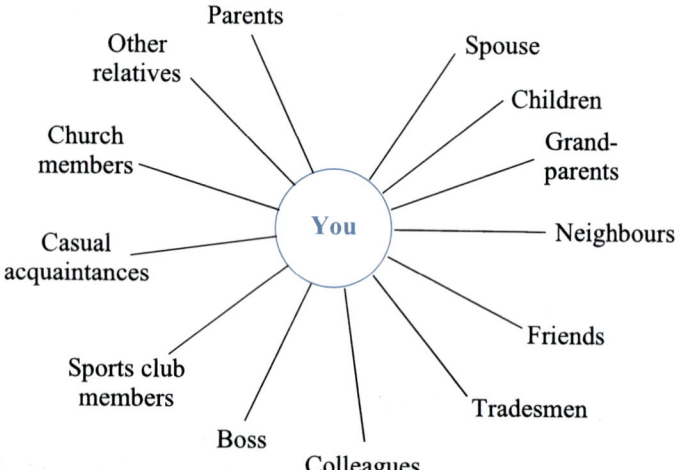

The role you play at any particular time will depend on what others expect of you, and what the circumstances are. For example, if you work with someone whom you also happen to know socially, you will probably play the role of 'colleague' while at work and that of 'friend' at other times.

Activity 7

■ Time guide 3 minutes

Using the chart above, list *five* or *six* other roles you might play.

_____

_____

_____

_____

_____

_____

You may have written down:

■ husband (or wife);

■ parent;

■ boss;

■ subordinate;

■ child;

■ neighbour;

and so on.

4.2
Role signs

To help clarify the roles we have, role signs are often used.
One common role sign is the dress we wear.

● In many places of work it is easy to distinguish between managers and workers of lower status, because the managers wear suits while shop-floor workers are in overalls.

● A nurse in a hospital and a security guard both wear uniforms as role signs.

Another kind of role sign is location.

● We assume that someone behind a counter in a shop is a shop assistant.

● We hand over money to strangers quite willingly, just because they are behind the counter and glass screen of a bank.

Activity 8

■ Time guide 2 minutes

What role signs – if any – will you have as team leader?

_____

_____

_____

_____

■ A team leader or supervisor sometimes wears a different colour uniform, or no uniform when the team members do wear one.

■ Another form of role sign is just being able to stand and watch while others work and adopting a 'look of authority'.

■ An office or a desk can act as a role sign, also.

It's useful to realise what your role signs are. Perhaps you have to get used to them in order to live up to the part.

Now we'll look at some sources of stress caused by the roles people play. Although names are given for each condition, this is done mainly to distinguish one source of role stress from another. You don't have to worry about remembering the names used.

**4.3
Role ambiguity**

If you aren't certain about some aspect of the role you are meant to be playing, you may well become confused and inefficient.

Suppose your boss tells you she is unhappy about the amount of litter in the car park and tells you to 'sort it out'.

What are you meant to do?

● Act in the role of hygienist, and get the litter picked up?

● Act in the role of disciplinarian and reprimand the people who drop litter?

● Act as liaison officer and report the matter to Security?

Of course, a situation like this would only cause you temporary uncertainty. However, if you are generally unsure of your role at work the consequences can be more damaging – to you, to the organisation or both.

We can call uncertainty about roles *role ambiguity*.

As a team leader, it is largely up to you to define the job-related roles of team members and to ensure there is no role ambiguity.

Activity 9

■ Time guide 4 minutes

Have you ever been uncertain about any aspect of your role or position at work? One example is being unsure about what was expected of you in terms of performance; perhaps your boss didn't make clear the standard of work required.

What form did your own role uncertainty take? What did you do about it? (Answer these questions briefly.)

_____

_____

_____

_____

_____

_____

You may have had an experience of:

- being uncertain about just what your responsibilities were in a certain situation – say, one day when you were left in charge without specific instructions;

- working for someone who wasn't consistent about the standards demanded or the method of assessment to be used;

- not knowing how you could make progress or advance your position – say, a situation where promotion was only possible if someone left the organization.

This reminds us of one of the team leader's responsibilities:

a team looks to its leader for clarity and consistency.

**4.4
Role conflict and
role incompatibility**

Imagine holding a meeting of your workteam, where you are playing the role of chairman or team leader, when your mother unexpectedly walks into the room. What is your role now?

In a situation like this, where what is expected of you in one role clashes with what is expected in another role, you can be said to be in *role conflict*.

A similar condition occurs where the expectations of your role are different in different people; this is known as *role incompatibility*.

Team leaders may often find themselves in role conflict or role incompatibility. Very commonly, the team expect one kind of behaviour, while the team leader's boss expects another.

Activity 10

- Time guide 3 minutes

Can you recall an occasion when your team or your colleagues had different expectations of you from your boss? What was the outcome?

_____

_____

_____

_____

_____

It's sometimes very hard to please everybody. Typically:

- the team may be looking to you for increased financial rewards and the boss talks only in terms of economy and efficiency;

- your colleagues want you to slow down whereas the boss wants you to speed up;

- or perhaps your image as a friendly easy-going team leader is in conflict with the role you have to play when holding a disciplinary interview.

Role incompatibility can also occur where your own standards don't agree with the organization's standards, or where the image you have of yourself doesn't coincide with other people's. You could imagine a soldier who is told to shoot into a rioting mob being under great stress through role incompatibility.

You may want to try to avoid the stress caused by role conflict or incompatibility by:

● sticking to your principles of integrity and not being compromised;

● separating your life into compartments: evenings and weekends for your social life, daytime for work life, for example;

● being yourself - people will learn from your behaviour what to expect from you.

**4.5
Role overload**

It isn't unknown for people to have to take on numerous roles at the same time. A familiar example is the housewife; a typical housewife has the multiple roles of: cleaning lady, nurse, mother, washerwoman, lover, driver, counsellor, hostess ... and so on. If you are or have been a housewife, you may care to complete the list yourself!

Having too many roles can lead to *role overload*, which is really an exaggerated form of role conflict. The team leader may be in danger of suffering from this condition.

Activity 11

■ Time guide 3 minutes

You may feel that you have too many roles to play in your job. What can anyone suffering from role overload do about it? Try to suggest *two* things.

_____

_____

_____

_____

If you are already a team leader you are probably already coping with a number of different roles, some of which will conflict. What most people have to do is:

■ decide priorities, by assigning levels of importance;

■ delegate certain roles to others;

■ perhaps agree with the boss that some roles be removed from the job specification.

**4.6
Role underload**

The opposite of role overload is *role underload*. It occurs when an individual feels that he or she is capable of more roles or a bigger role.

It also can be stressful, because it affects self-image. People doing jobs which they feel are below their capabilities will be dissatisfied and probably inefficient.

The organization can unwittingly make things worse by telling employees how capable they are and what great prospects they have, and then proceeding to ask them to play very junior and undemanding roles. This can have the effect of making people feel very dissatisfied.

Activity 12

Part

A

■ Time guide 3 minutes

Suppose you take over a new team and you feel that some of the members are probably being under-utilised. Due to the limitations of the job, there isn't a great deal of scope for expanding roles. How might you tackle this situation?

Write down your answer briefly, after a few minutes' thought.

_____

_____

_____

_____

_____

You may have suggested:

■ assigning roles which match capabilities wherever possible;

■ encouraging good work and effort, without building unrealistic hopes or promising opportunities which may not be realised;

■ perhaps talking to your fellow supervisors to see whether reassigning some members to other teams would be possible and beneficial to all concerned.

You may agree that role underload is probably just as common as role overload. These are the kind of problems that are a challenge to the team leader. The first step is *identifying* what the problem is. The second is ***doing something about it***.

5　　　　　　Managing

A team leader is a manager. Managers have to work with and through other people to get a job done.

This means that, in common with any other manager, the team leader must

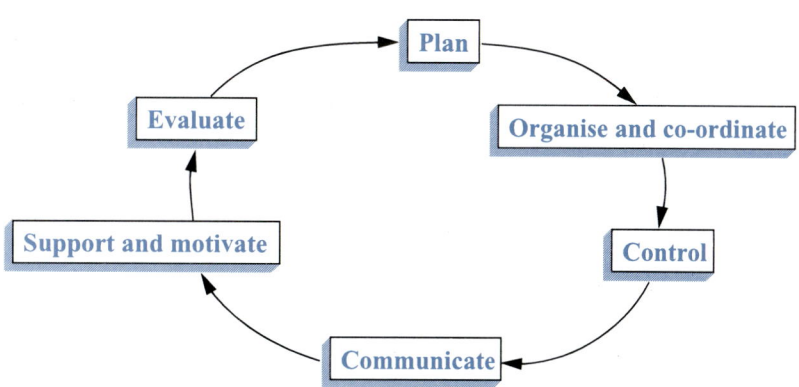

Planning consists of deciding what has to be done and working out how to achieve it.

There are several levels of planning in an organisation.

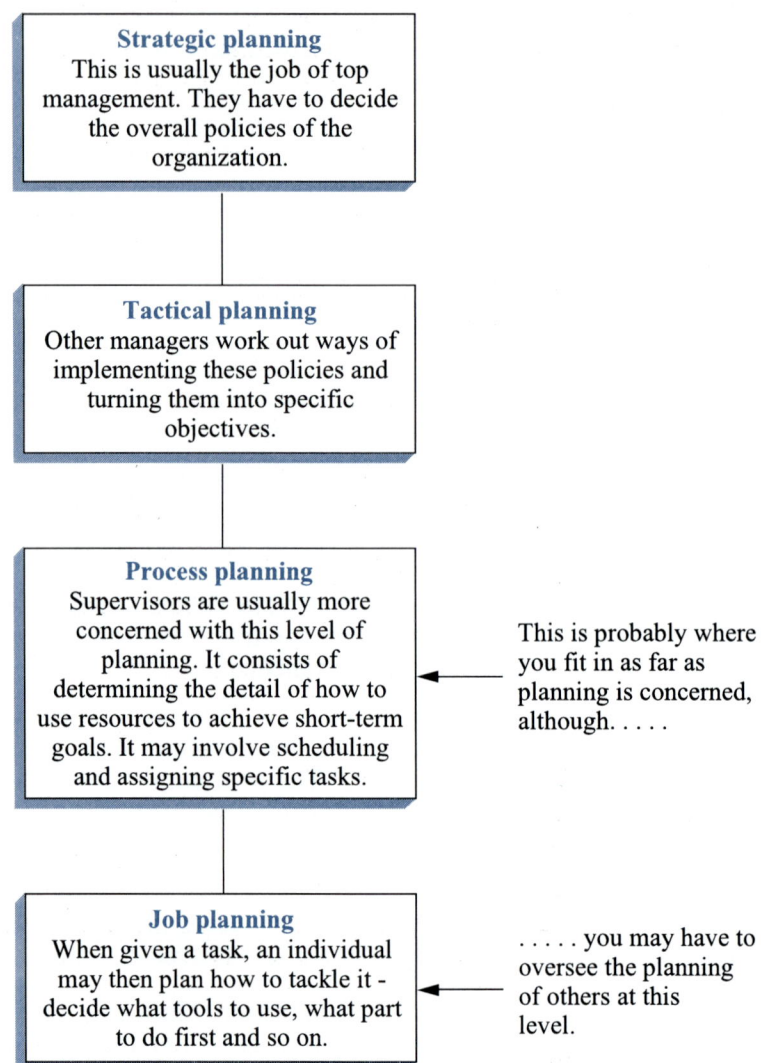

Strategic planning
This is usually the job of top management. They have to decide the overall policies of the organization.

Tactical planning
Other managers work out ways of implementing these policies and turning them into specific objectives.

Process planning
Supervisors are usually more concerned with this level of planning. It consists of determining the detail of how to use resources to achieve short-term goals. It may involve scheduling and assigning specific tasks.

This is probably where you fit in as far as planning is concerned, although. . . . .

Job planning
When given a task, an individual may then plan how to tackle it - decide what tools to use, what part to do first and so on.

. . . . . you may have to oversee the planning of others at this level.

Activity 13

■ Time guide 5 minutes

How much planning do you do? When you are assigned a task, how do you decide the best way of doing it?

Do you start work, or assign the job to one of your team without further thought? Or do you carefully plan everything before you start: perhaps draw up a schedule, make calculations about the resources and the time required, write detailed specifications?

_____

_____

_____

_____

_____

_____

Do you ever get into difficulties through lack of planning and preparation? Should you be doing more planning? (If so, what is stopping you? What can you do about it?)

_____

_____

_____

_____

_____

_____

However you answered, you will no doubt agree that

good planning saves time and resources.

5.2
Organizing and co-ordinating

Organizing involves ensuring that all the required resources are in the right place at the right time.

These resources include human ones – the people who are to do the work and provide the supporting services.

Co-ordinating means harmonising the efforts of all participants in the enterprise.

A large part of a team leader's work is concerned with organising and co-ordinating. As with all management activities, it is only possible to organize and co-ordinate effectively with the co-operation of others. A supervisor relies on the team, other teams, other managers and other supervisors.

Activity 14

■ Time guide 6 minutes

Do you consider yourself to be a good organizer and co-ordinator? _____

What would help to improve your organizing or co-ordinating:

Better planning? ☐

Improved information from your boss? ☐

Improved information from your team? ☐

Improved information from other parts of the organization? ☐

Increased co-operation? ☐

Briefly describe a situation you've encountered recently where things weren't as well organized or co-ordinated as you would have wished.

_____

_____

_____

_____

_____

What action can you take to avert or ease the problem in the future?

_____

_____

_____

_____

_____

Of course, it's easy to blame others for not getting the job done.

We hear excuses like this all the time, don't we?

● 'If only I could get some co-operation around here...'

● 'If I were given the proper information in advance I'd be able to do my job properly.'

● 'I'm well organized – it's these other people.'

● 'There's no point in my team sweating blood when no one else is putting in any effort.'

The fact of the matter is that:

team leaders are charged with the job of making things happen.

Sitting back and blaming others gets us nowhere. What is needed is:

Planning,

Persistence,

Persuasiveness and

Perseverance.

**5.3
Controlling**

Controlling means ensuring that what you want to happen really is happening, and doing something about it if it isn't.

Activity 15

■ Time guide 3 minutes

There are several implications in this statement. For example, it implies that you know what you want to happen. What else does it imply? Can you think of *two* more things?

_____

_____

_____

The statement also implies that:

■ you know not only *what* you want to happen but *when* it should happen: these two things together mean that you have made a plan;

■ you will *realize* when the plan is or is not being adhered to;

■ if something is going wrong, you are able to understand *what* is going wrong;

■ if something is going wrong, you are able to make adjustments to help bring the plan back on course.

Activity 16

■ Time guide 6 minutes

Can you recall an incident when you seemed to lose control of a sequence of events? Describe what happened very briefly.

_____

_____

_____

_____

_____

Looking back, is there something you could have done differently, for example:

■ monitored an operation more closely;

■ checked the feedback information you were given;

■ been quicker to revise your plan in the light of events;

■ found a better method of measuring progress?

_____

_____

_____

Close control is another important element of the team leader's job. This doesn't necessarily mean standing over your team while they work. They need scope to apply their skills and develop their own individuality. It does mean having reliable feedback information and moving in to make corrections before it's too late.

**5.4
Communicating**

Many ventures fail because of poor communication. Communicating well with the team means:

● being clear in your own mind what you want;

● expressing your ideas in a format (language, formula, chart etc.) that will be understood;

● making sure that you really *are* understood.

Activity 17

■ Time guide 3 minutes

Suppose you give a complicated instruction to a member of your team. Suggest an action you might take to ensure that it will be understood.

_____

_____

_____

You may have suggested:

- asking the team member to repeat the instruction back to you;

- testing how much was understood, by asking questions about it;

- giving the team member time to digest the information, then holding a discussion about it.

The important point is *feedback*. Sometimes it simply isn't enough to ask: 'Did you understand that?' and get a nod of the head in reply. Sometimes that nod of the head means

- 'He'll think I'm stupid if I say I don't understand'; or

- 'I got the gist of it – I'll try and work out the rest later'; or

- 'If I say I understand, he might go away and leave me to think about something more interesting.'

Comprehension is confirmed by two-way communication.

**5.5
Supporting and
motivating**

Motivation means getting people to *want* to do a good job.

Activity 18

- Time guide 2 minutes

Which of the following do you think might be successful methods of motivating people at work?

- Saying 'Thank you' for a job well done. ☐

- Feeding back the results of work and its impact on the organisation and/or on the customer. ☐

- Threatening or bullying people. ☐

- Paying bonuses for increased effort or output. ☐

You may, quite reasonably, have ticked all four methods. However, threatening or bullying is not to be recommended, because it will almost certainly be counter-productive in the long run!

Sometimes a few words of thanks or praise may have a greater motivating effect than more complex methods. Letting the team members know the effects and results of their work can also sometimes improve the overall motivation dramatically.

Supporting the team includes:

- providing the facilities needed;

- providing the training needed;

- protecting the members from unwanted outside interference;

- showing trust;

- backing up the team when things go wrong.

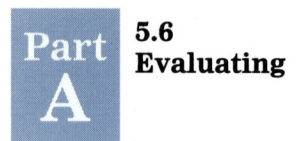
Evaluating is concerned with appraisal of performance and assessment of results.

Evaluation has to be a continuous activity, because it's part of the control process. However, it's important to carry out formal evaluation at appropriate and regular intervals, for the individual, for the team and for the task.

Activity 19

■ Time guide 4 minutes

Do you make a point of appraising the performance of your team at regular intervals?

Yes	No

If not, can you influence your organisation to introduce such a system?

_____

_____

_____

How are the results of the team's work assessed?

_____

_____

_____

_____

If you have experience of leading a team you will know that appraisal and assessment is much more difficult when you have no standards to measure against. Therefore, setting measurable targets is invariably a good idea, if it is possible.

■ Time guide 12 minutes

Complete the following sentences with a suitable word or words.

1. As team leader, you have to get things done through _____ _____ rather than doing them _____.

2. Achievement of the _____ is the team leader's _____ responsibility.

3. The team leader has responsibilities towards the _____, the _____ and the _____.

4. Good planning saves _____ and _____.

5. Match the words listed with the correct description.

   PLANNING, ORGANIZING, CO-ORDINATING, CONTROLLING, EVALUATING, MOTIVATING.

   _____ means harmonising the efforts of all participants in the enterprise.

   _____ means ensuring that what you want to happen really is happening, and doing something about it if it isn't.

   _____ consists of deciding what you want to do and working out how to achieve it.

   _____ means getting people to want to do a good job.

   _____ involves ensuring that all the required resources are in the right place at the right time.

   _____ is concerned with appraisal of performance and assessment of results.

Which of the following statements are TRUE and which are FALSE?

6. The role a person plays at any particular time depends on that person, not what other people expect. TRUE/FALSE

7. An organisation chart defines all the important relationships within an organisation. TRUE/FALSE

8. If you are uncertain about the role you are playing, you may be confused and the job may suffer. TRUE/FALSE

9. One way to deal with having conflicting roles is to separate your life into compartments. TRUE/FALSE

Select the TWO correct statements from the list below.

10. The team leader's responsibilities include:

    (a) assessing individual performance;

    (b) defining his or her own role in the organization;

    (c) explaining the group task to members of the team;

    (d) trying to overcome the problems of role overload and to try to achieve a condition of role underload.

Response check 1

1. As team leader, you have to get things done through OTHER PEOPLE, rather than doing them YOURSELF.

2. Achievement of the TASK is the team leader's MAIN responsibility.

3. The team leader has responsibilities towards the TASK, the TEAM and the INDIVIDUAL.

4. Good planning saves TIME and RESOURCES.

5. The correct matches are:

   CO-ORDINATING means harmonising the efforts of all participants in the enterprise.

   CONTROLLING means ensuring that what you want to happen really is happening, and doing something about it if it isn't.

   PLANNING consists of deciding what you want to do and working out how to achieve it.

   MOTIVATING means getting people to want to do a good job.

   ORGANIZING involves ensuring that all the required resources are in the right place at the right time.

   EVALUATING is concerned with appraisal of performance and assessment of results.

6. The role a person plays at any particular time depends on that person, not what other people expect. This is FALSE: roles are very much dependent upon the expectations of others.

7. An organization chart defines all the important relationships within an organization. This is FALSE: many informal or 'unofficial' relationships are very important.

8. If you are uncertain about the role you are playing, you may be confused and the job may suffer. This is TRUE.

9. One way to deal with having conflicting roles is to separate your life into compartments. This is TRUE, especially if there is conflict between work roles and social or family roles.

10. The team leader's responsibilities include:

    (a) assessing individual performance;

    (c) explaining the group task to members of the team.

    Of the other two:

    (b) defining the team leader's role in the organization is really the job of his or her superior;

    (d) the team leader may struggle to overcome the problems of role overload but role underload is not really a desirable goal.

6   Summary

- As team leader, you have to get things done **through other people**, rather than doing them yourself.
- **Achievement of the task** is the team leader's main responsibility.
- The team leader is responsible for:

  - **the task**;

  - **the individual**;

  - **the team**.

- Sources of **role stress** include: role ambiguity; conflict of roles or incompatibility of roles; having too many roles resulting in role overload; role underload.

● Team Leading is *management* and management comprises of:

  – *planning* is deciding what has to be done and working out how to achieve it;

  – *organizing* is ensuring that all the required resources are in the right place at the right time;

  – *co-ordinating* is harmonising the efforts of all participants in the enterprise;

  – *controlling* is ensuring that what you want to happen really is happening, and doing something about it if it isn't;

  – *motivation* is getting people to *want* to do a good job;

  – *evaluating* is appraisal of performance and assessment of results.

1 Introduction

Some leaders are tall and muscular; others are small and petite. One leader may be outgoing and jolly, while another always looks serious. All leaders have their own individual personalities, styles and approaches to the task. Identifying the characteristics of leadership is not easy.

But there are many qualities which all leaders need. In this part of the workbook we'll be looking at what those qualities are. We'll be asking whether leadership can really be learned. Then we'll try to determine what a good leader should *be* and what a good leader should *do*.

2 Can leadership be learned?

Extension 2 John Adair's excellent book *Effective Leadership* is intended to be a self-development manual for leaders and potential leaders.

Activity 20

■ Time guide 4 minutes

An overheard conversation:

'Leaders are born with special qualities. Some people stand out from the crowd. You've either got it or you haven't.'

'Nonsense. Anyone can become a leader. It's a skill and can be learned like any other.'

Do you agree with either of these arguments? Give a brief reason for your answer.

_____

_____

_____

I would be more inclined to support the second speaker.

Of course, we have all read about people with outstanding leadership qualities. You may have even been lucky enough to have known someone who could inspire great loyalty and respect in others.

History tells us of remarkable leaders. Some examples which come to mind are Napoleon, Churchill, the Duke of Wellington and George Washington. Each made a mark by leading his countrymen in famous ventures. Perhaps you have your own heroes or heroines. (There are other great leaders we might not wish to emulate because they have used their leadership qualities for evil ends – like Hitler and Stalin, for instance.)

However, most leaders are not born with special qualities – they learn leadership. Think of the leaders of industry and commerce – the supervisors and managers. They are mostly people who have started out in junior positions and have learned the skills of leadership as they have progressed.

Now read the following account and then note down what you think about it.

Activity 21

■ Time guide 5 minutes

Milly Covacic was a trained laboratory technician and had been doing the same kind of work for five years, since she left college. She worked for a large chemical company and Milly was respected by others in the department for her first class workmanship. She was naturally a quiet person, but she was pleasant enough and enjoyed her job.

One day the workteam supervisor left and Milly was offered the post. She didn't give it much thought, and, because the money was better, she accepted straight away.

When she started her new job, Milly found it very hard not to carry on working in the way she had before. She knew it was up to her to manage the rest of the team, but whenever she saw someone doing a job badly she took over the work herself – it was easier than trying to get other members of the team to do it better.

When the department manager found out what was going on, she wasn't at all pleased. 'You have to ask yourself whether you really want to be a supervisor, Milly, or a technician. You can't carry on in the same way as before if you are in charge.'

Milly has to ask herself some searching questions. Suggest **two** things she should be deciding in her own mind.

_____

_____

_____

_____

How you respond to this Activity will depend upon what kind of person you are. A decision has to be made, nevertheless. Milly has to ask herself what she wants:

■ Does she really want to be a supervisor?

■ Has she the ambition and desire, apart from wanting the extra money?

■ Does she have the confidence in herself to tackle the job?

If she does, she has to learn to act like a leader. This means a complete re-think of her approach to the job. She might reasonably ask her boss for training and advice.

So this is the most basic qualification for becoming a leader. To learn to manage a team you must have a real commitment to the job and must have belief in yourself.

> To be a leader you have to want to be one
> and believe in your own ability to be one.

Activity 22

■ Time guide 2 minutes

Of course, Milly starts with one important advantage which will help her in her role of supervisor. Can you see what it is?

_____

_____

_____

Milly is a skilled technician, which means she will know the work of the other technicians well. She will be able to help them and guide them – though hopefully not to the extent of taking over the work! More importantly, she will be able to **spot quickly when things are going wrong**.

She will be respected for her knowledge, which will give her more authority.

To be a good leader it helps to be experienced in the work.

3   What are the qualities of a good leader?

How can we identify the characteristics of effective leadership? If we think about the enormous range of situations in which leaders are found, it is difficult to see how it is possible to sum up what makes a good leader in a few words. Take these three cases, for example:

Frank was a passenger on a ship which hit a freighter and started to sink. Many people on board panicked, but Frank kept calm and helped the crew organize lifeboats. Then he took the lead in getting other passengers to safety. When they all got to dry land, Frank was praised for his presence of mind and leadership qualities.

Mark was a team leader of aircraft mechanics in his country's air force. During an emergency operation, it was the job of Mark's team to keep the aircraft flying. This involved long, painstaking work under trying conditions. A single mistake could have caused an aeroplane to crash, which would have jeopardised the whole mission. When the operation was over, Mark's commanding officer congratulated him on his devotion to duty and remarkable leadership.

Bettina led a team of computer operators employed by a large company which had worked away steadily for several years. The quality of the team's work was consistently high, staff turnover low and the team the envy of many other supervisors. Bettina's leadership qualities were recognised and, when a vacancy arose, she got promoted to departmental manager.

It's easy to spot the **differences** between the three cases.

For instance, Frank, unlike the other two, wasn't even an appointed leader and yet took charge when an emergency situation arose.

Both Mark and Bettina led a team; Mark had to inspire his mechanics to put in a supreme effort during a limited exercise. In Bettina's case, although conditions weren't particularly arduous, she set herself the task of maintaining very high team standards over a long period.

Part B

Activity 23

> ■ Time guide 4 minutes
>
> What characteristics were common to the three leaders above? Jot down *two* or *three* features which apply to all three cases.
>
> _____
>
> _____
>
> _____
>
> _____

You may have noted that all three leaders must have had:

■ **skills at dealing with people**. They each had to influence others, which means they had to have tact and diplomacy. One can imagine too, especially in Frank's case, how the leaders would have to be polite yet firm in getting people to do what they wanted;

■ **the ability to inspire confidence**, by setting an example and/or by imposing high standards;

■ **managing skills**, including the ability to organise and co-ordinate, to communicate well and to support and motivate;

■ **sound personal qualities** for others to believe in them and want to follow them;

■ a great deal of **determination**.

Activity 24

> ■ Time guide 4 minutes
>
> Are there any other characteristics displayed by effective leaders, which we haven't mentioned? Think of the day-to-day running of a workteam, or think instead of any leader you particularly respect and admire. What other qualities does a team look for in a team leader? Try to list *two* points.
>
> _____
>
> _____
>
> _____

You may have included such leadership characteristics as:

- *dependability* – never letting the team down;

- *integrity* – being uncompromising in keeping to a set of values;

- *fairness* – not taking sides, but dealing with people in an even-handed way;

- *being a good listener* – rather than trying to dominate discussions;

- *consistency* – not changing values or rules to suit the circumstances;

- *having a genuine interest in others* – liking people and identifying with them;

- *having confidence in the team* – believing in the team, which will in turn give the team confidence;

- *giving credit where it's due* – rather than claiming credit for the leader;

- *standing by the team when it's in trouble* – and not trying to disclaim responsibility for the problems;

- *keeping the team informed* – and not hiding behind a 'cloak of mystery'.

Generally, also, good leaders have *a history of success and achievement*.

In summary, we can separate the skills and qualities of an effective leader into four groups:

- *managing skills* – ability to organize, co-ordinate, communicate and motivate;

- *people skills* – ability to negotiate and to influence others; tact, firmness with courtesy, adaptability, a genuine interest in others;

- *personal qualities* – integrity, dependability, loyalty to the team and the organization, fairness and impartiality, persistence and determination;

- *personal achievements* – a history of success and personal growth.

Activity 25

> ▦ Time guide 2 minutes
>
> (a) In your experience, do leaders usually have *all* these skills, qualities and achievements? | Yes | No |
>
> (b) Do you know any effective leader who has *none* of them? | Yes | No |

You may not know anyone who has all these attributes. Many leaders, in my experience, are strong in some qualities and weaker in others. On the other hand, it would be hard to think of a leader who didn't possess at least some of them.

Activity 26

■ Time guide 3 minutes

We've listed a lot of leadership attributes. Are there any which strike you as being difficult for an aspiring leader to acquire? To take a couple of examples, can someone really learn to be 'dependable' or 'fair'? Briefly jot down any views you have.

_____

_____

_____

_____

_____

Well, I've never heard of any training school with 'dependability' or 'fairness' or 'integrity' on the curriculum! You could argue that these kinds of attributes are part of a person's character – you are either dependable or you aren't, for instance. But experience tells us that this isn't all of the truth. Often, it isn't until people are put into a situation where others depend upon them that they display such qualities.

Now let's look at the behaviour demanded of a leader.

4   What does a leader have to do?

Here's another case history which illustrates some important points about leadership.

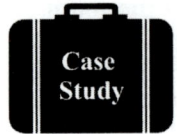

Case Study

Since Gerry had been appointed as team leader things hadn't gone too well. He talked over his problems with Des, his friend.

'Ever since I've taken this job, I've got nothing but earache from the boss. Every time something goes wrong in the team, he comes to me to complain. I don't see why I should put up with it. I just come here to do a day's work, like anyone else. If somebody messes things up, I don't see why I should take the blame.'

'But you told me the other day that you had been congratulated when your team managed to get that shipment off to Austria, Gerry.'

'Ah, yes, well that was largely due to me, so I deserved the pat on the back. But if I tell someone in the team to do something and they forget or slope off to lunch early, I'm not going to defend them. I can only control my own actions, not anyone else's.'

Activity 27

■ Time guide 4 minutes

How do you see Gerry's problems? If you were his friend, what could you say to him? Put your ideas down briefly in the space below.

_____

_____

_____

_____

As I see it, Gerry is feeling the burden of responsibility and doesn't much like it. He is happy enough to accept the praises when things go well, but doesn't seem to want to be blamed for the team's actions when something goes wrong. Unfortunately, a leader can't act like that.

> The team leader has to accept responsibility for the team.

This implies an attitude of mind.

> A leader must feel personally responsible for the team and all its resources, including the people.

Taking on a team means that, from day one, you are answerable for all its members' actions at work. Quite a responsibility!

But there's even more to it than that. The team won't always behave as you would like it to. There will be times when team members will let you down. Yet you can't afford to let the team down. If the team fails then you fail. There's no future in trying to dissociate yourself from the shortcomings of the team.

Gerry, in the case above, did not seem prepared to defend his team's behaviour to management. If he acts like this, he should not be surprised if his managers take the attitude that:

● Gerry's team have been misbehaving, so Gerry is not running the team very well;

● Gerry is not standing up for his team members, so he is not loyal to his team.

> The team leader always has to represent the team well to management.

We can learn one more lesson from Gerry's case.

Even when things go badly, the leader must remain committed to the team and enthusiastic about its good qualities.

> The team leader has to be fully committed and enthusiastic.

Now let's turn our attention to the information the leader has to give to the team, so that it can function effectively.

First and foremost, the team needs to know its overall objectives – what it is aiming at.

> The team needs to know its purpose.

The aims and objectives may be something which never vary, such as: 'The aims of this team are to clean the windows of all the buildings belonging to the XY Corporation regularly every two months, to a high standard.'

Alternatively, the aims and objectives may have to be restated as the job changes, as with a team of trouble-shooters, for example, which has to tackle new problems from week to week.

Whatever the aims and objectives are, **it is important to state them and make them clear to the team**.

What other kind of general information is useful to the team?
One clue is given in the following account.

The Bramley Machinery Company made fail-safe devices for electrical equipment. One day last year they were awarded a large contract by a South American government for the supply of some of their devices, which were to be installed in very difficult environmental conditions, to safeguard electrical power equipment. This was only a small part of a huge project.

Ken Waterson, Bramley's Sales Manager, travelled several times to South America to demonstrate the equipment and eventually to sign the contract. While he was there he was given brochures which described the government project and the part it would play in building up the prosperity of the country.

On returning to England, Ken showed the brochures to the company directors. The board decided that they would ask Ken and his staff to put on a special presentation for all the company workforce, showing what the project was all about, and the small but vital contribution to it being made by the Bramley equipment.

Activity 28

■ Time guide 3 minutes

Do you think that this kind of information is useful to staff members whose job has nothing to do with selling or contracts? What effect do you think this had on the people who were working on the equipment concerned? Jot down your views briefly.

_____

_____

_____

_____

Many would agree that this kind of background information, although it seems to have little to do with engineering, manufacturing or many of the other activities in a company will actually be very helpful. Knowing something about how your work affects other people, other companies and other countries can be a very positive motivating factor.

People like to know

- 'What effect is my work – and my team's work – having on other people?'
- 'Where does it fit in with the rest of the organization?'
- 'What happens to the goods we produce – who uses them?'
- 'Is the user (or the customer) happy with the work our team does?'
- 'What does the rest of the organization we work for get up to?'
- 'Are our team objectives being met?'

This can be summed up by saying,

the team needs feedback.

Activity 29

■ Time guide 3 minutes

Now let's think about the consideration the leader has to give to individuals in the team.

Imagine you are a member of a well-run, enthusiastic and successful team. So far so good. But you have your own problems and your own ambitions. You aren't just a member of the team, you're an individual. You want to develop your own abilities and perhaps you have ambitions to be a team leader yourself one day.

With this in mind, what do you look for in your team leader? Jot down your ideas, briefly.

_____

_____

_____

_____

Surely, as an individual, you need:

■ to have your abilities and your contribution to the team recognised;

■ scope to develop;

■ understanding of your needs and feelings.

We can summarise this by saying that

the team leader has to be aware of the needs of every team member and provide scope for individual expression and development.

■ Time guide 10 minutes

Complete the following sentences with a suitable word or words.

1. To be a leader you have to _____ to be one and believe in your own _____ to be one.

2. The team leader has to accept _____ for the team.

3. The team needs to know its _____ – what it is aiming at.

4. The team leader has to be aware of the _____ of every team member and provide scope for individual expression and _____ .

Which of the following statements are TRUE and which are FALSE?

5. All leaders need skills at dealing with people and should enjoy working with people. TRUE/FALSE

6. All leaders must be physically strong, so as not to be intimidated. TRUE/FALSE

7. No leader can be expected to remain enthusiastic and positive when the team performs consistently badly. TRUE/FALSE

8. The primary set of information needs of the team is its aims and objectives. TRUE/FALSE

9. Which six of the following ten characteristics are recognised as being most important in good leadership?

Dependability
Height
Ability to listen
Good communication skills
Integrity
Extrovert personality
High intelligence
Ability to inspire confidence
Methodical approach
Good managing skills

Response check 2

1. To be a leader you have to WANT to be one and believe in your own ABILITY to be one.

2. The team leader has to accept RESPONSIBILITY for the team.

3. The team needs to know its PURPOSE – what it is aiming at.

4. The team leader has to be aware of the NEEDS of every team member and provide scope for individual expression and DEVELOPMENT.

5. All leaders need skills at dealing with people and should enjoy working with people. This is TRUE.

6. All leaders must be physically strong, so as not to be intimidated. This is FALSE: physical strength is not necessary.

7. No leader can be expected to remain enthusiastic and positive when the team performs consistently badly. This is FALSE: the performance of the team depends largely on the performance of the leader. Enthusiasm and a positive outlook are part of the requirements of a leader.

8. The primary set of information needs of the team is its aims and objectives. This is TRUE.

9. The following characteristics are seen most often in good leaders. The other characteristics listed may sometimes be seen, but do not seem to be as important.

Dependability
Ability to listen
Good communication skills
Integrity
Ability to inspire confidence
Good managing skills

5   Summary

- To be a leader you have to want to be one and believe in your ability to be one.

- To be a good leader it helps to be experienced in the work.

- The skills and qualities of leadership can be separated into four broad categories:

  - *managing skills*: ability to organize, co-ordinate, communicate and motivate;

  - *people skills*: ability to negotiate and to influence others; tact, firmness with courtesy, adaptability, a genuine interest in others;

  - *personal qualities*: integrity, dependability, loyalty to the team and the organization, fairness and impartiality, persistence and determination;

  - *personal achievements*: a history of success and personal growth.

- The team leader has to accept responsibility for the whole team.

- The team leader has to represent the team well to management.

- The team leader has to be fully committed and enthusiastic.

- The team leader has to make the objectives clear and provide feedback to the team.

- The team leader has to be aware of the needs of every team member and provide scope for individual expression and development.

TEAM BUILDING AND LEADING

1   Introduction

No team stays the same for very long. Changes are taking place continually. People leave and new members join; even the leader is replaced from time to time. There is a process of continuous building and development going on.

In this part of the unit, we will trace the development of a new team. (If you are the newly appointed leader, any team is certainly 'new' in the sense that it will go through a process of upheaval, as if it was newly formed.)

Writers in this field have identified four distinct stages of team development:

> forming, storming, norming and performing.

We will look at each of these stages to see what goes on in them and to look at what actions the team leader can take to help guide the team through them.

2   Forming

The time of formation of a team is one of exploration and uncertainty. It is therefore important that the leader gives a clear lead and lays down firm targets and guidelines.

> At the forming stage the team looks to the leader
> for standards, targets and guidance.

2.1
Team selection

Activity 30

> ▪ Time guide 4 minutes
>
> Assuming that you have the opportunity to influence the selection of the team, what qualities would you look for in a new team member? Try to write down *two* basic criteria which are important in team selection.
>
> _____
>
> _____
>
> _____

Probably the first consideration in selecting a team member is whether he or she can do the job. You have to look for someone with:

> competence in the field of work.

Perhaps equally important is the ability of members to work together, so the:

aptitude to work with the rest of the team

is a second criterion during the selection process.

This doesn't mean that everyone must have the same kind of personality – a mix of personalities is probably best. However, you certainly don't want people who will be 'troublemakers' and upset the rest of the team. Nor do you want anyone who isn't prepared to 'pull their weight', to contribute to the best of their abilities.

These are the two essential qualities which any team leader would be wise to look for: the ability to do the job and the ability to fit into the team. When it comes to what might be called personal attributes, some useful questions to bear in mind are whether the potential team member

● has a sense of humour;

● is realistic about his or her strengths and weaknesses;

● has worked successfully in a team in the past;

● appears to have integrity.

Team members should be selected on
their competence, ability to fit in and personal attributes.

2.2
Setting up good communication channels

At the team forming stage, the team leader must also bear in mind the necessity for good lines of communication. It is during this phase that it may be possible to tackle any problems of communication that may exist.

Activity 31

■ Time guide 3 minutes

What barriers to good communication might exist – between team members, between the leader and the team, or between the team and the rest of the organization? Try to list *two* barriers.

_____

_____

_____

_____

Some barriers you may have thought of are:

■ noise;

■ working in the open air;

■ having to wear helmets or ear protection;

■ physical separation between members, or an isolated team, working away from the rest of the organisation;

■ a team leader who sits in an office well away from the team;

■ jargon or technical language which not everyone can understand;

■ members having limited knowledge of English;

■ inability of some members to read or write;

■ members or teams who won't communicate with others.

A special kind of communication problem can occur when every member of the team works separately, away from the others. This situation is seen more frequently nowadays, because of the trend towards 'telecommuting' or 'home networking', whereby people are employed from home, using modern technology to communicate with the office.

Because good communication is so vital to the effectiveness of a team, the team leader must make every effort to overcome any difficulties as soon as they arise.

**2.3
Getting the
team involved**

At the earliest possible stage, the team leader needs to encourage team cohesiveness and to promote a sense of team identity and purpose. An important approach to achieving this is to get the members of the team involved in:

● *planning*,

● *organizing* and

● *evaluating*.

Activity 32

◼ Time guide 3 minutes

How do you get the team involved in planning, organizing and evaluating? What could you do to encourage involvement? List *two* or *three* ideas, if you can.

_____

_____

_____

_____

Among the things you could do are to:

◼ ask the members' opinions: show that you value their views on what is to take place;

◼ seek their advice and specialized knowledge: one person can't appreciate all aspects of any matter – often members of your team will be more experienced or better informed than you are, especially in their specialist areas;

◼ allow them to take part in making decisions: this increases involvement provided the problem is not trivial or insoluble.

Decision-making is a process of:

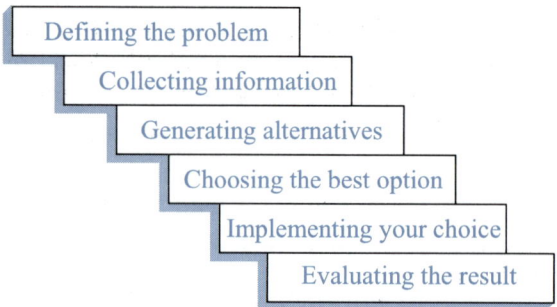

- Defining the problem
- Collecting information
- Generating alternatives
- Choosing the best option
- Implementing your choice
- Evaluating the result

■ encourage them to assess their own performance and the performance of the team as a whole. Suitable questions are:

– 'Did we reach the target/objectives?'

– 'If not, why not?'

– 'If yes, what did we do that we can repeat?'

– 'How well did we work as a team?'

**2.4
Encouraging
team identity**

Activity 33

■ Time guide 3 minutes

Aside from what we've already discussed, how else would you go about encouraging team identity? What could you do, as team leader, to generate a feeling of comradeship and belonging? Try to note *two* things.

_____

_____

_____

_____

What you are trying to do is to encourage an attitude of mind, so that the members *think of themselves as part of a team*.

■ The *words* you use would be important here: saying 'we' and 'us' rather than 'I' and 'me'.

■ You would also want to advocate *sharing* – of jokes, of resources, of problems, of triumphs and so on.

■ You might feel it important to create opportunities for *informal social activity* at work – without necessarily encroaching on members' leisure time.

■ Having *a team name and 'home base'* are also important to the team identity.

During the storming phase of team development team members are in conflict. This conflict mainly stems from the uncertainty felt by the members as they 'find their feet'.

It is also a period of discovery.

Activity 34

■ Time guide 4 minutes

What are the members trying to discover when they form into a team? List **three** things.

_____

_____

_____

_____

Individuals are trying to discover, among other things:

■ their place in the team;

■ their relationships with other members;

■ the ways in which they will be expected to behave;

■ the scale and complexity of the task;

■ the information and resources they will need to cope;

■ the best approach to the task;

■ their relationship with the leader.

**3.1
How the conflict
may show itself**

Activity 35

■ Time guide 3 minutes

How is this conflict likely to show itself, do you think? Jot down your ideas, briefly.

_____

_____

_____

_____

The conflict may be open and obvious: disagreement and argument among the members, which in extreme cases may lead to personal hostility and aggression. There may well be a division into two or more 'sides', each representing certain opinions.

The conflict also takes place within the minds of individuals and the symptoms may therefore not be so obvious:

■ nervousness;

■ a reluctance to get down to the job;

■ sullenness;

■ spending excessive amounts of time on trivial tasks;

■ not taking part in group discussions.

These may all be signs of a lack of an individual's ability to get to grips with the real issues.

3.2
How to cope

Activity 36

■ Time guide 3 minutes

How can you, the leader, best cope with the storming stage? Write down *two* or *three* ideas for dealing with it.

_____

_____

_____

_____

You may agree that among the best methods for dealing with the uncertainty and conflict of the storming stage are to:

■ set an example by showing that you have confidence, clear ideas and are determined for the team to succeed;

■ clarify every question raised, if there is a straightforward answer;

■ encourage open, democratic discussion of any issues which are divisive, not allowing bullying or 'blackmail' but bringing out all the arguments;

■ summarise the arguments once discussion has taken place and, if possible, get the whole group to decide;

■ emphasise the importance of the task and of working together to achieve it;

■ keep conflict focused on the job, rather than on personalities;

■ avoid win/lose situations;

■ guide and support individuals who take time to settle down.

Activity 37

■ Time guide 4 minutes

What about those situations where it is hard to reach agreement?

Can you think of a situation in which you were involved, where the team was divided over some issue?

How was it handled?

■ Did the leader force through a decision?

■ Was the problem avoided or 'smoothed over' – perhaps to emerge again later?

■ Was a compromise solution reached?

■ Did the issue get resolved by 'give and take' – a kind of negotiated solution?

■ In some other way?

_____

_____

_____

_____

_____

_____

Sometimes the leader has to force a decision if a reasonable attempt to reach agreement has failed. The danger here is that there will be resentment leading to further repercussions.	Avoiding, ignoring or smoothing over seldom solves anything, because it may simply postpone the problem.
A compromise solution may be achievable, but the result may not please anyone.	Ideally, everyone will collaborate to reach a solution. This can take time, but may produce a good result.

4 Norming

A norm can be defined as *a standard of behaviour which is derived from what the members of the group perceive as being acceptable and appropriate*.

The norming stage is the period where the members of a group are beginning to work and act like a team. Standards are being set, in terms of:

● the methods of approach to the task;

● social behaviour;

● the roles to be played by individual members.

This stage is reached when the members have confidence in the team and the contributions they are to make.

■ Time guide 3 minutes

How would you expect this confidence to show itself? List *two* ideas.

_____

_____

_____

You may have noted that the members' confidence might show itself in:

■ a willingness to listen to the opinions of others;

■ a pride in the team;

■ genuine cohesiveness and a readiness to share;

■ mutual support;

■ a readiness to get on with the job.

The main danger, as group standards are established, is that norms might not be compatible with the aims and objectives of the organization. A team leader must be aware of this.

Now is not the time to relax,
but to press on with achieving the task.

5 Performing

The performing phase, as the name suggests, is the time when the team begins to produce useful work. The conflict is over, the members have settled into their roles and the constructive work on the task commences.

Activity 39

■ Time guide 2 minutes

Having steered the team through the difficult earlier stages, what more is there for the leader to do? Select *one* phrase from the list below.

– Sit back and reap the rewards. ☐

– Give encouragement, but largely let the team get on with it. ☐

– Work just as hard as before. ☐

There is only one answer here: having got the team over the forming, storming and norming stages, the team leader must work just as hard as before at:

■ monitoring the output and quality of the work, to ensure it meets targets;

■ ensuring performance is maintained;

■ seeking new challenges and targets, so that performance can be improved.

The Super Series unit on *Workteams* stated that **'a team which is not developing is stagnating'**.

Good teams are always striving to reach their peak. This can be observed in the very best sports teams. Other sides have a good season and get over-confident: the manager relaxes, the players look for rewards, perhaps the team even starts breaking up. The best teams win consistently, because they are never quite satisfied with their performance.

Winning next time is more important than winning last time.

The team leader's role is to:

- draw out the best from the team members;
- set ambitious but achievable targets;
- encourage effort but discourage complacency.

Most of all, the leader must lead by example – setting and maintaining high personal standards. That's what leadership is mostly about.

6   Co-ordinating with other teams

No team works in isolation. Even a team of Arctic explorers must maintain good contact and good relations with its supporting services.

A workteam cannot afford to become detached or aloof from the rest of the organization. That's why it is so important for the team leader to encourage a spirit of co-operation.

Activity 40

✉ Time guide 3 minutes

Can you think of a way in which a workteam might become isolated?

_____

_____

_____

- It is natural for a workteam to want to be to some extent independent and not to have to rely too much on others. This could in some cases be taken too far and lead to a kind of self-sufficiency: 'We don't need anyone to help us – we can manage on our own.'

- A team that is very cohesive – whose members are very close-knit – may put up barriers to 'outsiders'.

- Another reason why a team might become cut off from the rest of the organization is that communications are poor. A team separated by geographical distance may lose touch with 'base', for example. Communications problems of any kind may cause difficulties in maintaining good working relationships between different parts of the same organization.

Activity 41

Time guide 10 minutes

What other teams, sections, departments or key personnel are important to your team in achieving its targets?

_____

_____

_____

_____

What do you need from them and they from you?

_____

_____

_____

Do you think that your team's relationships with these people are good enough in all cases?

Yes	No

Do you think that your team's communications with these people are good enough in all cases?

Yes	No

What can you do to improve relationships and/or communications:

Holding meetings? _____

_____

Reports from you or from them? _____

_____

Sharing of information by including the other group on memos and reports?

_____

_____

New or modified procedures? _____

_____

Temporary lending/borrowing of people, so that each team gets to understand more about the other? _____

_____

Holding presentations or 'open days' of the work you do or the work they do?

_____

_____

Informal get-togethers? _____

_____

Whatever your answers, you may want to bear in mind that, as a leader, you owe allegiance to the organization you work for, as well as to your workteam. Don't forget that you are a member of this larger team and depend on support from your colleagues, just as they may feel they have a right to expect help from you.

Part C

Self check 3

■ Time guide 10 minutes

Complete the following sentences with a suitable word or words.

1. Select team members on their _____, ability to fit in and _____ attributes.

2. An important approach to getting the team more involved is: _____, organising and _____.

3. The norming stage is not the time to _____, but to press on with achieving the _____.

4. Winning _____ time is more important than winning _____ time.

Which of the following statements are TRUE and which are FALSE?

5. In selecting a new team, it's best to get people with the same kind of personalities and the same levels of competence. TRUE/FALSE

6. During the storming stage, members are trying to discover their role in the team. TRUE/FALSE

7. In resolving serious disagreement, the leader's job is to smooth things over, so that the problem is forgotten about. TRUE/FALSE

8. During the performing stage, the leader's job is to monitor output and maintain standards. TRUE/FALSE

9. Select the *one incorrect* statement from the list below:

   In dealing with the storming stage, the leader should:

   (a) emphasise the common task;

   (b) focus on personalities, rather than the conflict;

   (c) encourage discussion, giving everyone a chance to speak;

   (d) show confidence in the team.

53

Part C

Response check 3

1. Select team members on their COMPETENCE, ability to fit in and PERSONAL attributes.

2. An important approach to getting the team more involved is: PLANNING, organizing and EVALUATING.

3. The norming stage is not the time to RELAX, but to press on with achieving the TASK.

4. Winning NEXT time is more important than winning LAST time.

5. In selecting a new team, it's best to get people with the same kind of personalities and the same levels of competence. This is FALSE: it's best to get a mix of personalities and people with the competence to do the job.

6. During the storming stage, members are trying to discover their role in the team. This is TRUE.

7. In resolving serious disagreement, the leader's job is to smooth things over, so that the problem is forgotten about. This is FALSE: unresolved problems are seldom forgotten.

8. During the performing stage, the leader's job is to monitor output and maintain standards. This is TRUE.

9. The one *incorrect* statement is that, in dealing with the storming stage, the leader should:

(b) focus on personalities, rather than the conflict.

Focusing on personalities usually results in adding fuel to the flames, as the conflict becomes personal. The leader would do better to focus attention away from personalities and towards the task.

---

7   Summary

- The *forming* stage of team development is one of exploration and uncertainty. A clear lead and firm targets are needed.

- Team members should be selected on their *competence* to do the job, their ability to *fit in* and their *personal attributes*.

- An important approach to the task of increasing team cohesiveness and sense of identity is to get members involved in *planning*, *organizing* and *evaluating*.

- During the *storming* stage of team development, the members are in *conflict*.

- In order to cope with the *uncertainty* and conflict of the storming stage the leader should show *confidence*, give a clear lead and emphasise the importance of the team's task.

- The *norming* stage is the period when the members of the group are beginning to work and act like a team.

- The *performing* stage is the time when the team beings to produce useful work. For the leader the emphasis changes to *monitoring*, *maintenance* and promoting *higher standards*.

- *Co-ordination* and *co-operation* with other groups in the organization are essential. The team leader has to make sure good *relationships* and good *communications* are established and maintained.

1   Quick quiz

Well done – you have completed the unit. Now listen to the questions on Side one of the audio cassette. If you are not sure about some of the answers, check back in the workbook before making up your mind.

Write down your answers in the space below.

1 _____

_____

2 _____

_____

3 _____

_____

4 _____

_____

5 _____

_____

6 _____

_____

7 _____

_____

8 _____

_____

9 _____

_____

10 _____

_____

11 _____

_____

12 _____

_____

13 _____

_____

14 _____

_____

15 _____

_____

2   Action check

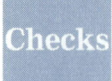

On Side two of the audio cassette, you will hear some discussions about team leading.

Listen carefully to the extracts, then try to answer the questions.

Write your answers and comments in the spaces below.

Situation 1:

_____

_____

_____

_____

_____

_____

Situation 2:

_____

_____

_____

_____

_____

_____

Situation 3:

_____

_____

_____

_____

_____

_____

Situation 4: _____

_____

_____

_____

_____

_____

_____

---

3   Unit assessment

■ Time guide 60 minutes

Case Study

Read the following case incident and then deal with the questions which follow, writing your answers on a separate sheet of paper.

Desmond Jalland took over as supervisor of a training workshop which taught the job skills of the construction industry to unemployed people. He was promoted because he was good at his job and popular with the students. The workshop had limited resources, which meant that there were a lot of administrative duties which had to be undertaken by the instructors in addition to their teaching and demonstrating roles. Although five other instructors worked for him, Desmond felt obliged to take on all these extra tasks, as well as listening to students' problems, helping them to find jobs and so on. Far from helping him, the other instructors became rather critical of Desmond because he never seemed to have time for them and their needs. One instructor left, which gave Desmond a new problem of trying to find a replacement. The overall picture is one of a harassed, overworked supervisor, demanding students and rather disaffected staff.

Answer the following questions. You do not need to write more than two or three sentences for each answer.

1. When Desmond took on the job of supervisor, his boss told him he needn't change his way of working very much, because the school couldn't afford to have a supervisor who wasn't also an instructor. Do you think this was good advice, or should Desmond take a different approach to the job, even if he does have to spend a large part of his day instructing?

2. Is he suffering from role overload or just overwork?

3. Which management skills is Desmond neglecting, in your opinion?

4. If you were in Desmond's shoes, what would you do differently?

---

4   Work-based assignment

The time guide for this assignment gives you an approximate idea of how long it is likely to take you to write up your findings.

You will need to spend some additional time gathering information, perhaps talking to colleagues and thinking about the assignment. The result of your efforts should be presented on separate sheets of paper.

Time guide 60 minutes

Read through the Action Plan on page 61 and think how you can apply it to your own situation. Choose any *ten* of the questions on the Action plan and for each one:

- give *one* example of how this Action prompt applies to you;

- give *one* example of something you now plan to do which should help to improve your performance as a team leader.

You need only write two or three sentences for each example.

1   Return to objectives

Now that you have completed your work on this unit, let us review each of our unit objectives.

You should be **_better able to:_**

- identify your role in the organization and your relationship with others;

Understanding where you fit into the overall scheme of things is always important. I hope the unit has helped you to perceive your role as team leader more distinctly and to clarify your position in relation to others. Of course, your role will change as you grow into the job and as you develop as an individual. You will want to build upon your relationships with your team and with everyone in the organization.

- recognize and develop the management skills you need to lead a team;

We have seen that management comprises a number of skills, including planning, organizing, co-ordinating, controlling, communicating and motivating. Like any leader or manager you will be stronger in some of these areas than in others. Increasing your competence involves learning to recognise your own shortcomings and striving to improve your performance.

- assess your own leadership qualities and potential;

The first prerequisite of leadership is wanting to lead and believing that you can. Once you have passed this basic requirement, everything is possible. The full potential of any leader can only be realised 'under fire' – in other words, the best way to know how well you can lead is to put your leadership skills to the test in difficult conditions.

- lead your team effectively.

Leading effectively means applying the skills and techniques we have discussed in this unit. It also means getting to know your team well and motivating its members to give of their best. The Action Plan in this part of the unit is designed to reinforce the points made earlier, and to help you improve your and your team's effectiveness.

2   Extensions

Extension 1	Book:	_Effective Teambuilding_
	Author:	J. Adair
	Publisher:	Pan Books, London, 2nd edition 1987
Extension 2	Book:	_Effective Leadership_
	Author:	J. Adair
	Publisher:	Pan Books, London, 2nd edition 1988

In addition to these Extensions, you may be interested to watch a series of videos produced by The Open College entitled 'In Charge'. These illustrate a number of aspects of supervisory work.

Review

These Extensions and the videos can be taken up via your Support Centre. They will arrange for you to have access to them. However, it may be more convenient to check out the materials with your personnel or training people at work – they could well give you access. There are good reasons for approaching your own people as, by doing so they will become aware of your continuing interest in the subject and you will be able to involve them in your development.

Work out your own plan of action for developing your skills as a team leader by responding to the following check questions and picking up the ■ action prompts.

You may want to ask your friends or your team to help you do this.

Check questions

Your response and intended action

1 Are you fully committed to the role of team leader? Are you confident that you have what it takes to succeed in the job?

_____

_____

_____

■ *If you are not committed and confident, try to analyse why by talking about it with someone who knows you well.*

2 Are you clear about your position within your organization and your official links to others?

_____

_____

_____

■ *If you aren't, talk to your manager about it.*

3 Is the team task well defined so that you know your main responsibility?

_____

_____

_____

■ *Get the task defined - it's important to the team and to you.*

4 Is there any ambiguity or uncertainty about aspects of your role?

_____

_____

_____

■ *Identify any role problems. Take steps to get them cleared up if you can.*

5 Are the expectations of others in your role consistent and compatible with one another?

_____

_____

_____

■ *If they aren't, write the names of the people making any demands of you which are unrealistic and try to discuss it with them.*

6 Is the amount of planning you do appropriate to the task?

_____

_____

_____

■ *Try making more detailed plans and spending more time at the planning stage. Analyse the difference this makes.*

61

7 **Are there good channels of information between yourself and the team, so that your efforts to organize and co-ordinate are not impeded unduly?**

_____

_____

_____

■ *Good communication channels depend on good co-operation. Think about ways of improving communication.*

8 **Do you feel in control most of the time?**

_____

_____

_____

■ *When you have gone through a situation when you didn't feel in control, try to analyse the reasons.*

9 **Is the team well enough motivated?**

_____

_____

_____

■ *Motivation is not always easily achieved or maintained.*

10 **Do you honestly give it the support it deserves?**

_____

_____

_____

■ *Your team deserves the best. Don't let it down.*

11 **What is your own assessment of your qualities as leader? What is the assessment of your closest colleague?**

_____

_____

_____

■ *Go through all the qualities we listed in the workbook and give yourself marks out of ten. Then work out how you can improve on or compensate for any deficiencies you are aware of.*

12 **Do you feel personally responsible for the team and all of its resources, including the people?**

_____

_____

_____

■ *If you don't, it may not be your fault. The system under which you work may not encourage it. Nevertheless, it is accepted that good leaders always do feel personally responsible.*

13 **Do you consistently represent the team well to management?**

_____

_____

_____

■ *It is part of being loyal.*

14 Do you try to make yourself aware of the needs of every team member and provide scope for individual expression and development?

_____

_____

_____

■ *List all your team members. Then write down their motivations and their ambitions. If you can't complete this list, get help from the members.*

15 To what extent do you get the team involved in planning, organizing, evaluating and decision making?

_____

_____

_____

■ *If you aren't sure, ask the team members. Then work together on ways to get better involvement.*

16 To what extent do you actively promote team cohesiveness and identity?

_____

_____

_____

17 How well do you cope with conflict?

_____

_____

_____

■ *Read the workbook again on this topic.*

18 How do you and your team react to success: by becoming complacent – or by trying harder?

_____

_____

_____

■ *Remember that winning next time is more important than winning last time.*

19 How do you and your team react to failure: by becoming despondent – or by trying harder?

_____

_____

_____

■ *Use failure to strengthen bonds and increase resolve.*

20 Are you satisfied with your team's relationships with other teams?

_____

_____

_____

■ *List all the teams and individuals important to the team. Find ways of building better links.*